MAR   2011

D1200344

Soccer in Asia

By
Mike Kennedy
with Mark Stewart

NORWOOD HOUSE PRESS

Norwood House Press, P.O. Box 316598, Chicago, Illinois 60631

For information regarding Norwood House Press,
please visit our website at: www.norwoodhousepress.com or call 866-565-2900.

Photo Credits:
    All interior photos provided by Getty Images.
Cover Photos:
    Top Left: Sports Illustrated for Kids/TIME Inc.
    Top Right: AFP/Getty Images.
    Bottom Left: AFP/Getty Images
    Bottom Right: Panini.
The soccer memorabilia photographed for this book is part of the authors' collections:
    Page 10) Sanli: Futera FZ LLC.
    Page 12) Cha: Panini; Daei: Panini, Recber: Panini; Sun: Sports Illustrated for Kids/TIME Inc.
    Page 13) Hashemian: Mundocrom; Nakata: Futera FZ LLC; Nakamura: Panini; Park: Futera FZ LLC.

Special thanks to Ben and Bill Gould.
Special thanks to John Snyder and Todd Meinig.

Designer: Ron Jaffe
Project Management: Black Book Partners, LLC
Editorial Production: Jessica McCulloch
Special thanks to Ben and Bill Gould

LIBRARY OF CONGRESS CATALOGING-IN-PUBLICATION DATA
    Kennedy, Mike, 1965-
      Soccer in Asia / by Mike Kennedy, with Mark Stewart.
        p. cm. -- (Smart about sports)
      Includes bibliographical references and index.
      Summary: "An introductory look at the soccer teams and their fans of
    countries in Asia. Includes a brief history, facts, photos, records, and
    glossary"--Provided by publisher.
      ISBN-13: 978-1-59953-448-0 (library ed. : alk. paper)
      ISBN-10: 1-59953-448-7 (library ed. : alk. paper)
      1. Soccer--Asia--Juvenile literature. 2. Soccer teams--Asia--Juvenile
    literature. I. Stewart, Mark, 1960- II. Title.
      GV944.A78.K46 2011
      796.334095--dc22
                                        2010044553

Manufactured in the United States of America in North Mankato, Minnesota.
170N–012011

Contents

Words in **bold type** are defined on page 24.

South Korea
celebrates a goal.

Where in the World?

Asia stretches across thousands of miles. Most of the world's people live there. Millions of them play and watch soccer. In 2002, the **World Cup** was played in Asia for the first time.

Once Upon a Time

In China, boys and girls played forms of soccer more than 2,000 years ago. In Japan, soldiers played between battles in times of war. The first soccer **leagues** in Asia began almost 100 years ago.

Kunishige Kamamoto and Aritatsu Ogi were stars for Japan in the 1960s and 1970s.

Iran plays Germany at Azadi Stadium.

At the Stadium

Azadi Stadium in Iran is the third biggest soccer stadium in Asia. Azadi means freedom in the Persian language. Azadi Stadium is one of the loudest in the world.

Town & Country

Soccer stars such as Tuncay Sanli often play for a town and a country. In 2010, Sanli played for a team in England and also the **national team** of Turkey. England and Turkey are more than 1,500 miles (2,414 kilometers) apart.

Tuncay Sanli wears the uniform of his English team.

Shoe Box

The soccer collection on these pages belongs to the authors. It shows some of the top Asian soccer stars.

Cha Bum Kun

Striker • South Korea
Cha Bum Kun kicked the ball very hard. Fans called him "Cha-BOOM."

Ali Daei

Forward • Iran

Ali Daei was known as "The King." He scored more than 100 goals for Iran.

Rustu Recber

Goalkeeper • Turkey
Rustu Recber was Turkey's star during the World Cup in 2002.

Sun Wen

Striker • China
Sun Wen was one of the best scorers in women's soccer.

Vahid Hashemian

Striker • Iran
Fans will never
forget the exciting
goals scored by
Vahid Hashemian.

Hidetoshi Nakata

Midfielder • Japan
Hidetoshi Nakata
was named one
of the 100 best
players in history.

Shunsuke Nakamura

Midfielder • Japan
Shunsuke Nakamura
could make shots turn
left or right in the air.

Park Ji Sung

Midfielder • South Korea
Park Ji Sung became
famous playing for a
team in England.

Can't Touch This

Players can use their upper bodies to control the ball. They are not allowed to touch the ball with their arms or hands. When this happens, the other team is given a **free kick**.

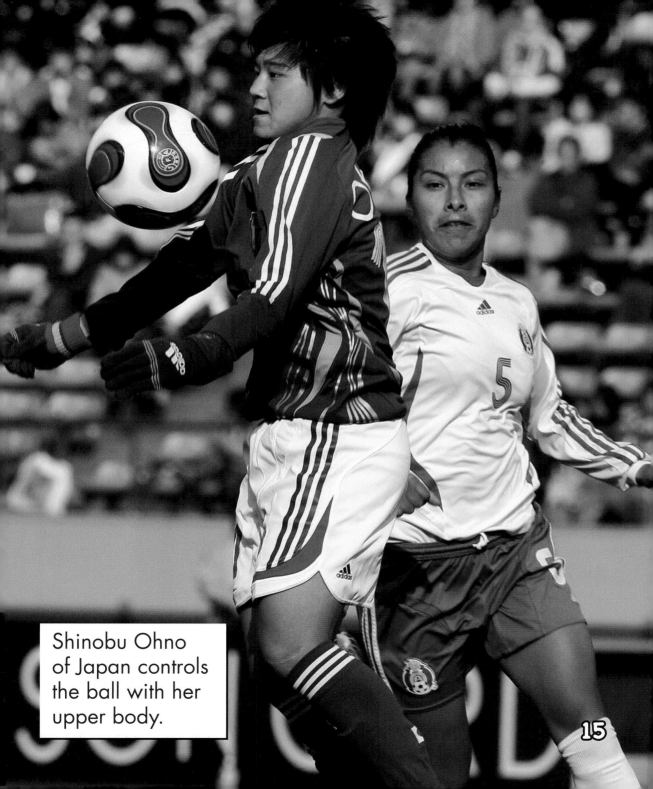

Shinobu Ohno
of Japan controls
the ball with her
upper body.

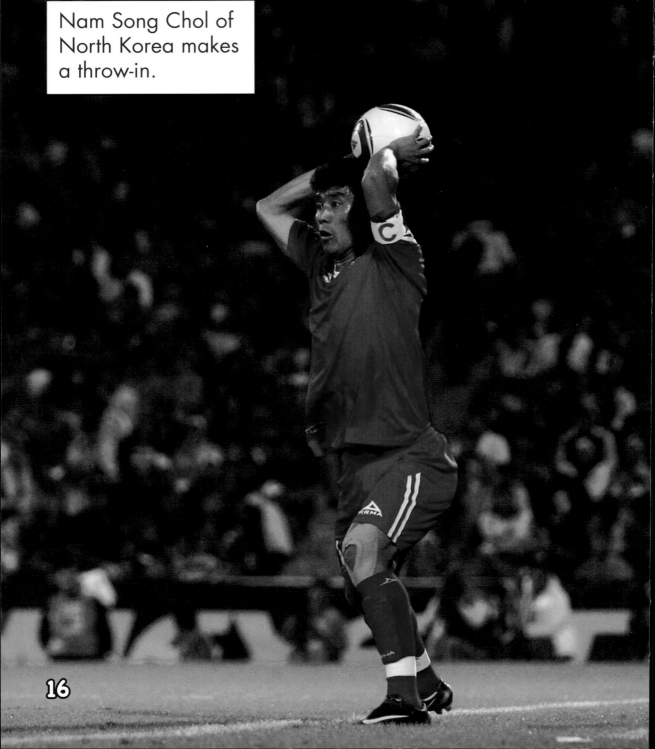

Nam Song Chol of North Korea makes a throw-in.

Just For Kicks

Watching soccer is more fun when you know some of the rules:

- Play stops when one team knocks the ball over the sideline on either side of the field.

- Play starts again with a "throw-in" by the other team.

- On a throw-in, you toss the ball to a teammate.

- You must use two hands. Your feet must stay on the ground.

17

On the Map

Girls and boys play soccer all over Asia, including these countries:

1. China
2. Iran
3. Iraq
4. Israel
5. Japan
6. Kuwait
7. Mongolia
8. North Korea
9. Saudi Arabia
10. South Korea
11. Turkey
12. Vietnam
13. Yemen

5 Japan

7 Mongolia

12 Vietnam

13 Yemen

Many countries have their own soccer stamps!

A soccer ball weighs about one pound (0.45 kilograms).

Stop Action

Soccer shoes are also called "boots."

Homare Sawa wears Japan's blue and white colors.

A soccer shirt is also called a "jersey."

21

We Won!

Asia has some of the best teams in the world!

Men's Soccer	Asian Cup* Champion
South Korea	1956 & 1960
Israel	1964
Iran	1968, 1972, & 1976
Kuwait	1980
Saudi Arabia	1984, 1988, & 1996
Japan	1992, 2000, & 2004
Iraq	2007

Women's Soccer	World Cup Runner-Up
China	2009

* The tournament that decides the Asian soccer champion.

Japan celebrates in 2004.

Soccer Words

FREE KICK
A shot given to a team after a foul has been called.

LEAGUES
Groups of teams that compete against each other.

NATIONAL TEAM
A team made up of players from the same country.

WORLD CUP
The tournament that decides the world champion of soccer. The World Cup is played every four years.

Index

Photos are on **bold** numbered pages.

Learn More

Learn more about the World Cup at www.fifa.com

Learn more about men's soccer at www.mlssoccer.com

Learn more about women's soccer at www.womensprosoccer.com